Copyright© 2020
by FMWNETWORK.COM
All rights reserved. No part of this book
be reproduced or used in any manner
whatsoever without written permission of
the copyright owner except for the use of
quotations in a book, articles, or reviews.

I dedicate this book to children around the world
who are victims of divorce.

Sometimes mom and dad cannot agree on many things. They can decide to separate. It is called divorce.

However, parents do not divorce their children. Parents and children do not agree on things sometimes, but parents and kids do not stop loving each other.

It's was a chilly, windy afternoon. Mom was reading while Drino and Trino were playing in the living room.

Dad joined them and said, "Drino and Trino, your mom and I have decided to get a divorce." "What? When? Why? Is it my fault"? Stammered Drino.

"It is neither you nor your sister's fault," replied dad. Dad continues. "This means your mom and I will not be staying together anymore. We have tried to work out our differences, but that has not worked. So, we have decided to separate for the good of the family."

"Your mom and I still love you, and we will always be there for you. However, some things will change. Weekdays you will spend with your mom;

While weekends and part of the holidays you will spend with me" concluded dad.

In Drino's thoughts, he still wondered if it was his fault that his parents were getting a divorce. That night before going to bed, he knelt and prayed to God to reunite his parents.

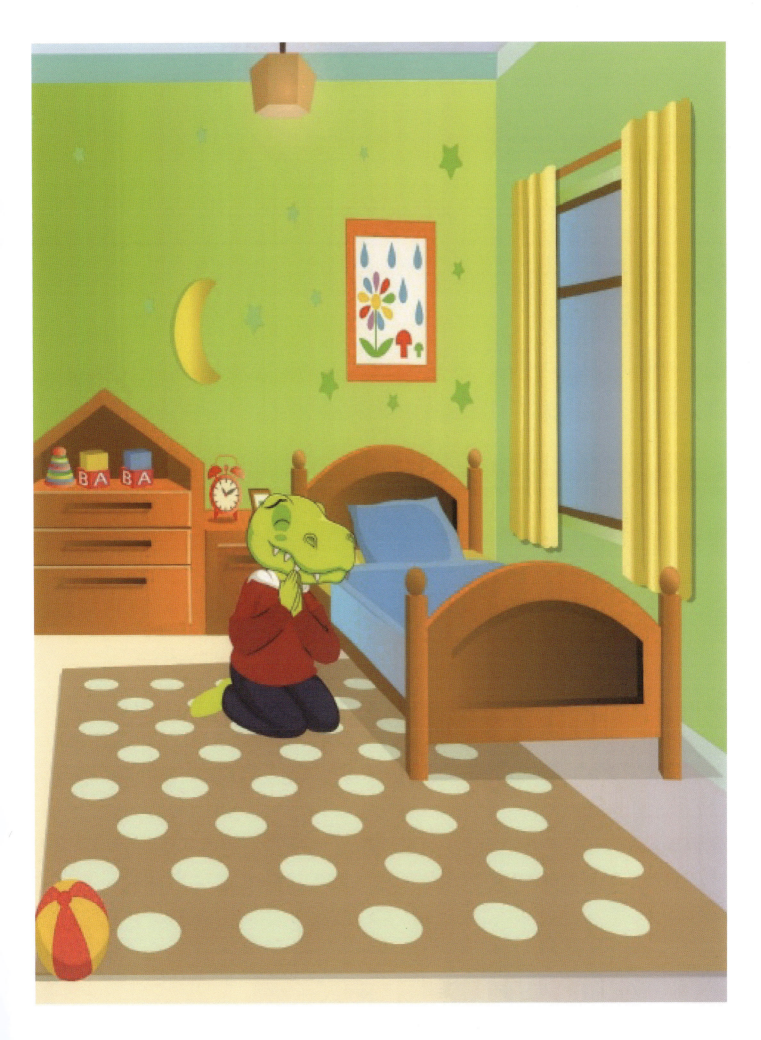

As Drino fell asleep, he talked to his friend Wise Turtle. "Wise Turtle, my parents are getting a divorce. Is it my fault or my sister's?" Wise Turtle responded. "Some parents divorce because they think they can do better when they live and do things separately. So, the divorce is not anyone's fault, especially you or your sister's. If someone tells you otherwise, then he or she is wrong! You must say it is not anyone's fault."

"I love both my dad and mom. I feel sad they do not agree with each other anymore. But do they still love us? " asked Drino.

Wise Turtle responded. "Your parents will always love you and your sister. Sometimes, your dad feels sad and worries you may not love him anymore, and your mom, too."

Drino grumbled about feeling frustrated, irritated, and angry after the news of his parent's divorce. "I feel sad and alone. Moreover, my parents sometimes argue. So I cry, and I do not want to go to school," complained Drino.

"Your parents will always love you, repeated Wise Turtle. They will always be there for you and your sister. Some parents divorce if they need to, but parents and their children do not divorce."

"I know my parents are divorcing because they do not agree anymore, and they should live and do things separately. But I feel like they do not care about our feelings. So I do not want to understand why my parents need to divorce right now," concluded Drino.

"It is okay to be angry towards your parents for separating, But, remember, there will be occasions when you also feel frustrated with your friends and peers. When this happens, move away and take a deep breath. Finally, you will get used to it and then realize it is not your fault," concluded Wise Turtle.

The sun was rising, and it was time for Drino to get ready for school. He got dressed and prepared his bag pack. The taught about his parents' divorce was not making him sad anymore as it was clear it was not his fault.

Throughout Drino's journey with his parents' divorce, he learned a lot. Most especially ways to cope. For example, he loves sports, so he joined the school soccer team because soccer makes him happy.

He also went to the school counselor whenever he needed help or someone to talk to. Drino has also talked to his parents, and he now understands why they are divorced. He also knows his parents still love him. Drino still feels frustrated sometimes, but he has learned ways to cope and be happy.

Ways To Cope With Parents Divorce.
- Tell Your Parents How You Feel.
- It Is Okay To Feel Frustrated Sometimes.
- Learn To Breathe To Calm Yourself.
- Ask For Help.
- Talk To Someone Other Than Your Parents Such As A Counselor.
- Get Involved In Activities You Love, (Sports, Music).

Daily Affirmations
- I Know Who I Am.
- I Have A purpose.
- I Am Strong.
- I Am Confident.
- It's Not My Fault.
- My Parents Love Me.
- We Are Still A Family.
- All Will Be Fine.

To find out more about when my next book
will be released,
Join our conversation on
Facebook:
https://www.facebook.com/groups/fm-wnetworkfamilycorner
Follow us on Instagram:
https://www.instagram.com/fortune_meli_wagoum/

Connect with us on LinkedIn:
https://www.linkedin.com/in/fortune-me-li-wagoum-941b1332/

Hope the book is helpful. Please tell me
what you think about it on Amazon

Printed in Great Britain
by Amazon

18574826R00022